50 Homemade Ice Cream Recipes

By: Kelly Johnson

Table of Contents

- Vanilla Bean Ice Cream
- Chocolate Chip Cookie Dough Ice Cream
- Strawberry Ice Cream
- Mint Chocolate Chip Ice Cream
- Coffee Ice Cream
- Salted Caramel Ice Cream
- Pistachio Ice Cream
- Chocolate Hazelnut Ice Cream
- Mango Sorbet
- Raspberry Sorbet
- Cookies and Cream Ice Cream
- Peanut Butter Cup Ice Cream
- Lemon Sorbet
- Coconut Ice Cream
- Cherry Garcia Ice Cream
- Almond Joy Ice Cream
- Tiramisu Ice Cream
- Chocolate Mint Ice Cream
- Brownie Batter Ice Cream
- Pumpkin Pie Ice Cream
- Cinnamon Ice Cream
- S'mores Ice Cream
- Lavender Honey Ice Cream
- Matcha Green Tea Ice Cream
- Birthday Cake Ice Cream
- Rocky Road Ice Cream
- Butter Pecan Ice Cream
- Blueberry Cheesecake Ice Cream
- Pina Colada Ice Cream
- Dulce de Leche Ice Cream
- Maple Walnut Ice Cream
- Tropical Fruit Ice Cream
- Mocha Ice Cream
- Peach Ice Cream
- Chocolate Churro Ice Cream

- Raspberry Chocolate Swirl Ice Cream
- Vanilla Custard Ice Cream
- Maple Bacon Ice Cream
- Black Forest Ice Cream
- Cherry Almond Ice Cream
- Green Tea Matcha Ice Cream
- Caramel Pretzel Ice Cream
- Coconut Chocolate Chip Ice Cream
- Brown Sugar Cinnamon Ice Cream
- Toffee Almond Ice Cream
- Honeycomb Ice Cream
- Gingerbread Ice Cream
- Chocolate Coconut Ice Cream
- Vanilla Bean Bourbon Ice Cream
- Apple Cinnamon Ice Cream

Vanilla Bean Ice Cream

Ingredients:

- 2 cups heavy cream
- 1 cup whole milk
- 3/4 cup granulated sugar
- 1 vanilla bean, split and scraped (or 1 tbsp vanilla extract)
- 5 large egg yolks
- Pinch of salt

Instructions:

1. **Prepare the Custard:** In a saucepan, combine the cream, milk, sugar, and vanilla bean seeds (or extract). Heat over medium until warm but not boiling.
2. **Whisk the Egg Yolks:** In a separate bowl, whisk the egg yolks. Gradually add a little of the warm cream mixture to temper the eggs, whisking constantly.
3. **Cook the Custard:** Pour the egg mixture back into the saucepan with the cream mixture. Cook over medium heat, stirring constantly, until the custard thickens enough to coat the back of a spoon.
4. **Cool and Churn:** Remove from heat, strain the custard to remove the vanilla bean pod, and let it cool to room temperature. Chill in the fridge for at least 2 hours, then churn in an ice cream maker according to the manufacturer's instructions.
5. **Freeze and Serve:** Transfer to an airtight container and freeze for at least 4 hours before serving.

Chocolate Chip Cookie Dough Ice Cream

Ingredients:

- 2 cups heavy cream
- 1 cup whole milk
- 3/4 cup granulated sugar
- 1 tsp vanilla extract
- 5 large egg yolks
- 1 cup mini chocolate chips
- 1/2 cup cookie dough (homemade or store-bought, cut into small pieces)

Instructions:

1. **Prepare the Custard:** Heat the cream, milk, and sugar in a saucepan until warm. In a separate bowl, whisk the egg yolks.
2. **Temper the Eggs:** Gradually add a little of the warm cream mixture to the yolks, whisking constantly, then pour the yolk mixture back into the saucepan.
3. **Thicken the Custard:** Cook over medium heat, stirring constantly, until the custard thickens. Remove from heat and cool to room temperature, then refrigerate until cold.
4. **Churn the Ice Cream:** Churn the custard in an ice cream maker. Once it starts to firm up, add in the cookie dough pieces and chocolate chips.
5. **Freeze and Serve:** Transfer to an airtight container and freeze for at least 4 hours before serving.

Strawberry Ice Cream

Ingredients:

- 2 cups heavy cream
- 1 cup whole milk
- 3/4 cup granulated sugar
- 1 tsp vanilla extract
- 2 cups fresh strawberries, pureed
- 1 tbsp lemon juice (optional)

Instructions:

1. **Prepare the Strawberry Puree:** Blend the strawberries in a blender or food processor until smooth. If desired, add a tablespoon of lemon juice to enhance the flavor.
2. **Prepare the Custard:** Heat the cream, milk, and sugar in a saucepan. In a separate bowl, whisk the egg yolks, then temper them with the warm milk mixture.
3. **Cook the Custard:** Cook over medium heat until thickened, then strain and chill in the fridge.
4. **Churn the Ice Cream:** Once cooled, add the strawberry puree and churn in an ice cream maker according to the manufacturer's instructions.
5. **Freeze and Serve:** Transfer to an airtight container and freeze for at least 4 hours before serving.

Mint Chocolate Chip Ice Cream

Ingredients:

- 2 cups heavy cream
- 1 cup whole milk
- 3/4 cup granulated sugar
- 1 tsp peppermint extract
- 5 large egg yolks
- 1/2 cup mini chocolate chips
- Green food coloring (optional)

Instructions:

1. **Prepare the Custard:** Heat the cream, milk, and sugar in a saucepan. In a separate bowl, whisk the egg yolks.
2. **Temper the Eggs:** Gradually add a little warm cream mixture to the yolks, whisking constantly, then pour the yolk mixture back into the saucepan and cook until thickened.
3. **Cool and Add Flavor:** Remove from heat, add the peppermint extract and a few drops of green food coloring (optional), and strain the custard.
4. **Churn the Ice Cream:** Once cooled, churn the mixture in an ice cream maker. Add mini chocolate chips when the ice cream is nearly frozen.
5. **Freeze and Serve:** Transfer to an airtight container and freeze for at least 4 hours before serving.

Coffee Ice Cream

Ingredients:

- 2 cups heavy cream
- 1 cup whole milk
- 3/4 cup granulated sugar
- 1 tbsp instant coffee or espresso powder
- 5 large egg yolks

Instructions:

1. **Prepare the Coffee Cream:** Dissolve the coffee or espresso powder in the warm milk and cream mixture, then heat until just warm.
2. **Make the Custard:** Whisk the egg yolks and gradually add the warm cream mixture. Return everything to the saucepan and cook over medium heat until thickened.
3. **Chill the Custard:** Strain the custard and let it cool completely before refrigerating for at least 2 hours.
4. **Churn the Ice Cream:** Churn the cooled custard in an ice cream maker according to the manufacturer's instructions.
5. **Freeze and Serve:** Transfer to an airtight container and freeze for at least 4 hours before serving.

Salted Caramel Ice Cream

Ingredients:

- 1 cup granulated sugar
- 2 tbsp unsalted butter
- 1 cup heavy cream
- 1 tsp vanilla extract
- 2 cups whole milk
- 3/4 cup granulated sugar
- 5 large egg yolks
- 1 tsp sea salt

Instructions:

1. **Make the Caramel:** In a saucepan, melt the sugar over medium heat, stirring constantly until it turns golden. Stir in the butter and then carefully add the cream. Remove from heat and stir in the vanilla extract and sea salt.
2. **Prepare the Custard:** In another saucepan, heat the milk and sugar until warm. Whisk the egg yolks and temper with the milk mixture, then cook until thickened.
3. **Combine the Caramel and Custard:** Mix the caramel sauce into the custard, strain, and let it cool.
4. **Churn the Ice Cream:** Churn the cooled mixture in an ice cream maker.
5. **Freeze and Serve:** Transfer to a container and freeze for at least 4 hours before serving.

Pistachio Ice Cream

Ingredients:

- 1 cup shelled pistachios, toasted
- 2 cups heavy cream
- 1 cup whole milk
- 3/4 cup granulated sugar
- 5 large egg yolks
- 1 tsp vanilla extract

Instructions:

1. **Prepare the Pistachio Paste:** Blend the pistachios in a food processor with a small amount of the milk until a smooth paste forms.
2. **Make the Custard:** Heat the cream, milk, and sugar until warm. Whisk the egg yolks and gradually add the warm mixture to the eggs.
3. **Cook and Cool the Custard:** Cook the custard until thickened, strain, and let cool to room temperature.
4. **Churn the Ice Cream:** Once cooled, add the pistachio paste and churn the mixture in an ice cream maker.
5. **Freeze and Serve:** Transfer to a container and freeze for at least 4 hours before serving.

Chocolate Hazelnut Ice Cream

Ingredients:

- 1 cup hazelnuts, toasted and chopped
- 2 cups heavy cream
- 1 cup whole milk
- 3/4 cup granulated sugar
- 5 large egg yolks
- 1/2 cup chocolate hazelnut spread (such as Nutella)

Instructions:

1. **Make the Hazelnut Custard:** Heat the cream, milk, and sugar until warm. Whisk the egg yolks and temper them with the warm cream mixture, then cook until thickened.
2. **Add the Hazelnut Spread:** Stir in the chocolate hazelnut spread until smooth, then strain the custard and let it cool.
3. **Churn the Ice Cream:** Once cooled, churn the custard in an ice cream maker, adding the chopped hazelnuts during the last few minutes.
4. **Freeze and Serve:** Transfer to an airtight container and freeze for at least 4 hours before serving.

Mango Sorbet

Ingredients:

- 4 ripe mangoes, peeled and diced
- 1/2 cup water
- 1/2 cup sugar
- 2 tbsp lime juice

Instructions:

1. **Prepare the Mango Puree:** Blend the mangoes in a food processor or blender until smooth.
2. **Make the Syrup:** Heat the water and sugar in a saucepan over medium heat until the sugar dissolves.
3. **Combine the Mango and Syrup:** Add the syrup and lime juice to the mango puree and blend until combined.
4. **Chill and Freeze:** Pour the mixture into an ice cream maker and churn according to the manufacturer's instructions. Transfer to an airtight container and freeze for at least 4 hours before serving.

Raspberry Sorbet

Ingredients:

- 4 cups fresh raspberries
- 1 cup water
- 1/2 cup sugar
- 1 tbsp lemon juice

Instructions:

1. **Prepare the Raspberry Puree:** In a blender or food processor, blend the raspberries until smooth.
2. **Make the Syrup:** In a small saucepan, combine water and sugar. Heat over medium heat until the sugar dissolves. Remove from heat and let cool.
3. **Combine and Strain:** Mix the raspberry puree with the syrup, then strain to remove the seeds.
4. **Chill and Freeze:** Add lemon juice, chill the mixture in the fridge, and churn in an ice cream maker according to the manufacturer's instructions.
5. **Freeze and Serve:** Transfer the sorbet to an airtight container and freeze for at least 4 hours before serving.

Cookies and Cream Ice Cream

Ingredients:

- 2 cups heavy cream
- 1 cup whole milk
- 3/4 cup granulated sugar
- 1 tsp vanilla extract
- 5 large egg yolks
- 15-20 chocolate sandwich cookies (like Oreos), crushed

Instructions:

1. **Prepare the Custard:** Heat the cream, milk, and sugar in a saucepan. Whisk the egg yolks, then gradually temper the yolks with the warm cream mixture.
2. **Cook the Custard:** Return everything to the saucepan and cook over medium heat, stirring constantly until the custard thickens. Strain the custard and let it cool to room temperature.
3. **Churn the Ice Cream:** Once cooled, churn the custard in an ice cream maker. Add crushed cookies when the ice cream starts to firm up.
4. **Freeze and Serve:** Transfer to an airtight container and freeze for at least 4 hours before serving.

Peanut Butter Cup Ice Cream

Ingredients:

- 2 cups heavy cream
- 1 cup whole milk
- 3/4 cup granulated sugar
- 1/2 cup peanut butter
- 5 large egg yolks
- 10-12 mini peanut butter cups, chopped

Instructions:

1. **Prepare the Custard:** Heat the cream, milk, and sugar in a saucepan. Whisk the egg yolks, then temper with the warm cream mixture.
2. **Cook the Custard:** Return the mixture to the saucepan and cook until thickened. Strain and cool to room temperature.
3. **Churn the Ice Cream:** Once cooled, churn the custard in an ice cream maker. Add chopped peanut butter cups when the ice cream is nearly firm.
4. **Freeze and Serve:** Transfer to an airtight container and freeze for at least 4 hours before serving.

Lemon Sorbet

Ingredients:

- 2 cups fresh lemon juice (about 8-10 lemons)
- 1 cup water
- 3/4 cup sugar
- 1 tbsp lemon zest

Instructions:

1. **Make the Syrup:** Combine the water and sugar in a saucepan. Heat over medium heat until the sugar dissolves. Let the syrup cool to room temperature.
2. **Mix the Lemon Juice:** Add the lemon juice and zest to the cooled syrup.
3. **Chill and Freeze:** Chill the mixture in the fridge for 1-2 hours, then churn in an ice cream maker according to the manufacturer's instructions.
4. **Freeze and Serve:** Transfer to an airtight container and freeze for at least 4 hours before serving.

Coconut Ice Cream

Ingredients:

- 2 cups heavy cream
- 1 cup coconut milk
- 3/4 cup granulated sugar
- 1 tsp vanilla extract
- 1/2 cup shredded unsweetened coconut (optional)

Instructions:

1. **Prepare the Custard:** Heat the cream, coconut milk, and sugar in a saucepan. Whisk the egg yolks, then temper with the warm mixture.
2. **Cook the Custard:** Return the mixture to the saucepan and cook until thickened. Strain and cool to room temperature.
3. **Churn the Ice Cream:** Once cooled, churn the mixture in an ice cream maker. Add shredded coconut (if using) when the ice cream is nearly firm.
4. **Freeze and Serve:** Transfer to an airtight container and freeze for at least 4 hours before serving.

Cherry Garcia Ice Cream

Ingredients:

- 2 cups heavy cream
- 1 cup whole milk
- 3/4 cup granulated sugar
- 5 large egg yolks
- 1 tsp vanilla extract
- 1 cup fresh cherries, pitted and chopped
- 1/2 cup chocolate chunks

Instructions:

1. **Prepare the Custard:** Heat the cream, milk, and sugar in a saucepan. Whisk the egg yolks and temper with the warm cream mixture.
2. **Cook the Custard:** Return the mixture to the saucepan and cook until thickened. Strain and cool to room temperature.
3. **Churn the Ice Cream:** Once cooled, churn the custard in an ice cream maker. Add cherries and chocolate chunks when the ice cream is nearly done.
4. **Freeze and Serve:** Transfer to an airtight container and freeze for at least 4 hours before serving.

Almond Joy Ice Cream

Ingredients:

- 2 cups heavy cream
- 1 cup whole milk
- 3/4 cup granulated sugar
- 1 tsp vanilla extract
- 1/2 cup sweetened shredded coconut
- 1/2 cup toasted almonds, chopped
- 1/2 cup chocolate chips

Instructions:

1. **Prepare the Custard:** Heat the cream, milk, and sugar in a saucepan. Whisk the egg yolks and temper with the warm mixture.
2. **Cook the Custard:** Cook until the mixture thickens, strain, and let it cool to room temperature.
3. **Churn the Ice Cream:** Once cooled, churn the mixture in an ice cream maker. Add coconut, almonds, and chocolate chips when the ice cream starts to firm up.
4. **Freeze and Serve:** Transfer to an airtight container and freeze for at least 4 hours before serving.

Tiramisu Ice Cream

Ingredients:

- 2 cups heavy cream
- 1 cup whole milk
- 3/4 cup granulated sugar
- 1 tbsp instant espresso powder
- 5 large egg yolks
- 1/2 tsp vanilla extract
- 1/2 cup mascarpone cheese
- 1/2 cup ladyfingers, crushed
- 2 tbsp coffee liqueur (optional)

Instructions:

1. **Prepare the Custard:** Heat the cream, milk, sugar, and espresso powder in a saucepan. Whisk the egg yolks and temper with the warm mixture.
2. **Cook the Custard:** Return the mixture to the saucepan and cook until thickened. Strain and let it cool.
3. **Churn the Ice Cream:** Once cooled, whisk in the mascarpone cheese and vanilla extract. Churn in an ice cream maker.
4. **Add Ladyfingers and Liqueur:** Add crushed ladyfingers and coffee liqueur (if using) when the ice cream starts to firm up.
5. **Freeze and Serve:** Transfer to an airtight container and freeze for at least 4 hours before serving.

Chocolate Mint Ice Cream

Ingredients:

- 2 cups heavy cream
- 1 cup whole milk
- 3/4 cup granulated sugar
- 1 tsp peppermint extract
- 1/2 cup chocolate chips or chunks
- 5 large egg yolks

Instructions:

1. **Prepare the Custard:** Heat the cream, milk, and sugar in a saucepan. Whisk the egg yolks and temper with the warm cream mixture.
2. **Cook the Custard:** Cook the mixture over medium heat until thickened. Strain and let cool to room temperature.
3. **Add Mint Flavor:** Stir in the peppermint extract once the custard is cooled.
4. **Churn the Ice Cream:** Churn in an ice cream maker. Add chocolate chips or chunks when the ice cream is nearly frozen.
5. **Freeze and Serve:** Transfer to an airtight container and freeze for at least 4 hours before serving.

Brownie Batter Ice Cream

Ingredients:

- 2 cups heavy cream
- 1 cup whole milk
- 3/4 cup granulated sugar
- 1 tsp vanilla extract
- 5 large egg yolks
- 1/2 cup brownie mix (unprepared)
- 1/2 cup mini chocolate chips or brownie pieces

Instructions:

1. **Prepare the Custard:** Heat the cream, milk, and sugar in a saucepan. Whisk the egg yolks, then temper with the warm cream mixture.
2. **Cook the Custard:** Return the mixture to the saucepan and cook until thickened. Strain and let it cool to room temperature.
3. **Make Brownie Batter:** In a bowl, mix the brownie mix with a small amount of milk to create a batter.
4. **Churn the Ice Cream:** Once the custard has cooled, churn it in an ice cream maker, adding the brownie batter in small spoonfuls as it starts to freeze.
5. **Add Chocolate Chips:** When the ice cream is nearly firm, fold in the chocolate chips or brownie pieces.
6. **Freeze and Serve:** Transfer to an airtight container and freeze for at least 4 hours before serving.

Pumpkin Pie Ice Cream

Ingredients:

- 2 cups heavy cream
- 1 cup whole milk
- 3/4 cup granulated sugar
- 1/2 cup pumpkin puree
- 1 tsp ground cinnamon
- 1/4 tsp ground nutmeg
- 5 large egg yolks
- 1 tsp vanilla extract

Instructions:

1. **Prepare the Custard:** Heat the cream, milk, and sugar in a saucepan. Whisk the egg yolks and temper with the warm cream mixture.
2. **Cook the Custard:** Return the mixture to the saucepan and cook until thickened. Strain and let it cool to room temperature.
3. **Add Pumpkin and Spices:** Once cooled, whisk in the pumpkin puree, cinnamon, nutmeg, and vanilla extract.
4. **Churn the Ice Cream:** Churn the mixture in an ice cream maker according to the manufacturer's instructions.
5. **Freeze and Serve:** Transfer to an airtight container and freeze for at least 4 hours before serving.

Cinnamon Ice Cream

Ingredients:

- 2 cups heavy cream
- 1 cup whole milk
- 3/4 cup granulated sugar
- 1 tsp ground cinnamon
- 5 large egg yolks
- 1 tsp vanilla extract

Instructions:

1. **Prepare the Custard:** Heat the cream, milk, sugar, and cinnamon in a saucepan. Whisk the egg yolks, then temper with the warm cream mixture.
2. **Cook the Custard:** Return the mixture to the saucepan and cook until thickened. Strain and let it cool to room temperature.
3. **Churn the Ice Cream:** Once the custard is cooled, churn it in an ice cream maker. Add the vanilla extract once the ice cream starts to firm up.
4. **Freeze and Serve:** Transfer to an airtight container and freeze for at least 4 hours before serving.

S'mores Ice Cream

Ingredients:

- 2 cups heavy cream
- 1 cup whole milk
- 3/4 cup granulated sugar
- 5 large egg yolks
- 1 tsp vanilla extract
- 1/2 cup graham cracker crumbs
- 1/2 cup mini marshmallows
- 1/4 cup chocolate chips

Instructions:

1. **Prepare the Custard:** Heat the cream, milk, and sugar in a saucepan. Whisk the egg yolks, then temper with the warm cream mixture.
2. **Cook the Custard:** Return the mixture to the saucepan and cook until thickened. Strain and let it cool to room temperature.
3. **Churn the Ice Cream:** Once the custard is cooled, churn it in an ice cream maker. Add graham cracker crumbs, mini marshmallows, and chocolate chips when the ice cream starts to firm up.
4. **Freeze and Serve:** Transfer to an airtight container and freeze for at least 4 hours before serving.

Lavender Honey Ice Cream

Ingredients:

- 2 cups heavy cream
- 1 cup whole milk
- 3/4 cup granulated sugar
- 1 tbsp dried lavender buds
- 5 large egg yolks
- 1/4 cup honey
- 1 tsp vanilla extract

Instructions:

1. **Infuse the Cream:** Heat the cream, milk, and sugar in a saucepan with the dried lavender buds. Allow it to steep for about 10 minutes, then strain.
2. **Prepare the Custard:** Whisk the egg yolks, then temper them with the warm lavender-infused cream mixture.
3. **Cook the Custard:** Return the mixture to the saucepan and cook until thickened. Strain and let it cool to room temperature.
4. **Add Honey and Vanilla:** Whisk in honey and vanilla extract once cooled.
5. **Churn the Ice Cream:** Churn in an ice cream maker according to the manufacturer's instructions.
6. **Freeze and Serve:** Transfer to an airtight container and freeze for at least 4 hours before serving.

Matcha Green Tea Ice Cream

Ingredients:

- 2 cups heavy cream
- 1 cup whole milk
- 3/4 cup granulated sugar
- 1 tbsp matcha green tea powder
- 5 large egg yolks
- 1 tsp vanilla extract

Instructions:

1. **Prepare the Custard:** Heat the cream, milk, and sugar in a saucepan. Whisk the egg yolks, then temper with the warm cream mixture.
2. **Dissolve the Matcha:** In a small bowl, whisk the matcha powder with a small amount of milk to make a smooth paste. Add it to the cream mixture.
3. **Cook the Custard:** Return the mixture to the saucepan and cook until thickened. Strain and let it cool to room temperature.
4. **Churn the Ice Cream:** Once cooled, churn in an ice cream maker. Add vanilla extract when it starts to firm up.
5. **Freeze and Serve:** Transfer to an airtight container and freeze for at least 4 hours before serving.

Birthday Cake Ice Cream

Ingredients:

- 2 cups heavy cream
- 1 cup whole milk
- 3/4 cup granulated sugar
- 5 large egg yolks
- 1 tsp vanilla extract
- 1/2 cup sprinkles
- 1/2 cup crumbled birthday cake (or cake mix)

Instructions:

1. **Prepare the Custard:** Heat the cream, milk, and sugar in a saucepan. Whisk the egg yolks, then temper with the warm cream mixture.
2. **Cook the Custard:** Return the mixture to the saucepan and cook until thickened. Strain and let it cool to room temperature.
3. **Churn the Ice Cream:** Once cooled, churn in an ice cream maker. Add sprinkles and cake crumbles when the ice cream is nearly frozen.
4. **Freeze and Serve:** Transfer to an airtight container and freeze for at least 4 hours before serving.

Rocky Road Ice Cream

Ingredients:

- 2 cups heavy cream
- 1 cup whole milk
- 3/4 cup granulated sugar
- 1 tsp vanilla extract
- 5 large egg yolks
- 1/2 cup mini marshmallows
- 1/2 cup chopped nuts (almonds or walnuts)
- 1/2 cup chocolate chips

Instructions:

1. **Prepare the Custard:** Heat the cream, milk, and sugar in a saucepan. Whisk the egg yolks, then temper with the warm cream mixture.
2. **Cook the Custard:** Return the mixture to the saucepan and cook until thickened. Strain and let it cool to room temperature.
3. **Churn the Ice Cream:** Once cooled, churn in an ice cream maker. Add marshmallows, nuts, and chocolate chips when the ice cream is nearly frozen.
4. **Freeze and Serve:** Transfer to an airtight container and freeze for at least 4 hours before serving.

Butter Pecan Ice Cream

Ingredients:

- 2 cups heavy cream
- 1 cup whole milk
- 3/4 cup granulated sugar
- 1/2 cup unsalted butter
- 1 cup pecans, toasted and chopped
- 5 large egg yolks
- 1 tsp vanilla extract

Instructions:

1. **Prepare the Custard:** Heat the cream, milk, and sugar in a saucepan. Whisk the egg yolks, then temper with the warm cream mixture.
2. **Cook the Custard:** Return the mixture to the saucepan and cook until thickened. Strain and let it cool to room temperature.
3. **Make the Butter Pecan Flavor:** In a separate pan, melt the butter and toast the pecans over low heat until fragrant. Let cool.
4. **Churn the Ice Cream:** Once cooled, churn in an ice cream maker, adding the toasted butter pecans once it starts to firm up.
5. **Freeze and Serve:** Transfer to an airtight container and freeze for at least 4 hours before serving.

Blueberry Cheesecake Ice Cream

Ingredients:

- 2 cups heavy cream
- 1 cup whole milk
- 3/4 cup granulated sugar
- 1 cup fresh or frozen blueberries
- 1/2 cup cream cheese, softened
- 5 large egg yolks
- 1 tsp vanilla extract
- 1/2 cup graham cracker crumbs

Instructions:

1. **Prepare the Blueberry Compote:** In a saucepan, heat the blueberries and sugar over medium heat until the blueberries break down and the mixture thickens. Let it cool to room temperature.
2. **Prepare the Custard:** Heat the cream, milk, and sugar in a saucepan. Whisk the egg yolks and temper with the warm cream mixture.
3. **Cook the Custard:** Return the mixture to the saucepan and cook until thickened. Strain and let it cool to room temperature.
4. **Add Cream Cheese:** Whisk the softened cream cheese into the cooled custard until smooth.
5. **Churn the Ice Cream:** Once the custard is cool, churn in an ice cream maker. Add the blueberry compote and graham cracker crumbs when the ice cream starts to firm up.
6. **Freeze and Serve:** Transfer to an airtight container and freeze for at least 4 hours before serving.

Pina Colada Ice Cream

Ingredients:

- 2 cups heavy cream
- 1 cup coconut milk
- 3/4 cup granulated sugar
- 1 cup pineapple chunks (fresh or canned)
- 1/2 cup shredded coconut
- 5 large egg yolks
- 1 tsp vanilla extract
- 1 tbsp dark rum (optional)

Instructions:

1. **Prepare the Pineapple:** Blend the pineapple chunks into a smooth puree and set aside.
2. **Prepare the Custard:** Heat the cream, coconut milk, and sugar in a saucepan. Whisk the egg yolks and temper with the warm cream mixture.
3. **Cook the Custard:** Return the mixture to the saucepan and cook until thickened. Strain and let it cool to room temperature.
4. **Add Coconut and Rum:** Stir in the shredded coconut, pineapple puree, and dark rum (if using) into the custard.
5. **Churn the Ice Cream:** Churn the mixture in an ice cream maker according to the manufacturer's instructions.
6. **Freeze and Serve:** Transfer to an airtight container and freeze for at least 4 hours before serving.

Dulce de Leche Ice Cream

Ingredients:

- 2 cups heavy cream
- 1 cup whole milk
- 3/4 cup dulce de leche
- 5 large egg yolks
- 1 tsp vanilla extract
- Pinch of salt

Instructions:

1. **Prepare the Custard:** Heat the cream and milk in a saucepan. Whisk the egg yolks and temper with the warm cream mixture.
2. **Cook the Custard:** Return the mixture to the saucepan and cook until thickened. Strain and let it cool to room temperature.
3. **Add Dulce de Leche:** Once the custard has cooled, whisk in the dulce de leche and vanilla extract until smooth.
4. **Churn the Ice Cream:** Churn the mixture in an ice cream maker.
5. **Freeze and Serve:** Transfer to an airtight container and freeze for at least 4 hours before serving.

Maple Walnut Ice Cream

Ingredients:

- 2 cups heavy cream
- 1 cup whole milk
- 3/4 cup maple syrup
- 1/2 cup toasted walnuts, chopped
- 5 large egg yolks
- 1 tsp vanilla extract

Instructions:

1. **Prepare the Custard:** Heat the cream, milk, and maple syrup in a saucepan. Whisk the egg yolks and temper with the warm cream mixture.
2. **Cook the Custard:** Return the mixture to the saucepan and cook until thickened. Strain and let it cool to room temperature.
3. **Churn the Ice Cream:** Churn the custard in an ice cream maker. Once it begins to firm up, add the toasted walnuts and vanilla extract.
4. **Freeze and Serve:** Transfer to an airtight container and freeze for at least 4 hours before serving.

Tropical Fruit Ice Cream

Ingredients:

- 2 cups heavy cream
- 1 cup coconut milk
- 1/2 cup diced pineapple
- 1/2 cup diced mango
- 1/2 cup diced papaya
- 3/4 cup granulated sugar
- 5 large egg yolks
- 1 tsp vanilla extract

Instructions:

1. **Prepare the Fruit Puree:** Blend the diced pineapple, mango, and papaya into a smooth puree. Set aside.
2. **Prepare the Custard:** Heat the cream, coconut milk, and sugar in a saucepan. Whisk the egg yolks and temper with the warm cream mixture.
3. **Cook the Custard:** Return the mixture to the saucepan and cook until thickened. Strain and let it cool to room temperature.
4. **Add Fruit Puree:** Once the custard has cooled, mix in the tropical fruit puree and vanilla extract.
5. **Churn the Ice Cream:** Churn in an ice cream maker according to the manufacturer's instructions.
6. **Freeze and Serve:** Transfer to an airtight container and freeze for at least 4 hours before serving.

Mocha Ice Cream

Ingredients:

- 2 cups heavy cream
- 1 cup whole milk
- 3/4 cup granulated sugar
- 2 tbsp instant coffee granules
- 5 large egg yolks
- 1 tsp vanilla extract
- 1/2 cup chocolate chips (optional)

Instructions:

1. **Prepare the Coffee:** Dissolve the instant coffee granules in 1/4 cup hot water and set aside.
2. **Prepare the Custard:** Heat the cream, milk, and sugar in a saucepan. Whisk the egg yolks and temper with the warm cream mixture.
3. **Cook the Custard:** Return the mixture to the saucepan and cook until thickened. Strain and let it cool to room temperature.
4. **Add Coffee and Chocolate:** Once the custard has cooled, whisk in the coffee mixture and vanilla extract. Fold in the chocolate chips (if using).
5. **Churn the Ice Cream:** Churn in an ice cream maker according to the manufacturer's instructions.
6. **Freeze and Serve:** Transfer to an airtight container and freeze for at least 4 hours before serving.

Peach Ice Cream

Ingredients:

- 2 cups heavy cream
- 1 cup whole milk
- 3/4 cup granulated sugar
- 2 large peaches, peeled and diced
- 5 large egg yolks
- 1 tsp vanilla extract

Instructions:

1. **Prepare the Peach Puree:** Blend the diced peaches into a smooth puree. Set aside.
2. **Prepare the Custard:** Heat the cream, milk, and sugar in a saucepan. Whisk the egg yolks and temper with the warm cream mixture.
3. **Cook the Custard:** Return the mixture to the saucepan and cook until thickened. Strain and let it cool to room temperature.
4. **Add Peach Puree:** Once cooled, mix the peach puree and vanilla extract into the custard.
5. **Churn the Ice Cream:** Churn in an ice cream maker according to the manufacturer's instructions.
6. **Freeze and Serve:** Transfer to an airtight container and freeze for at least 4 hours before serving.

Chocolate Churro Ice Cream

Ingredients:

- 2 cups heavy cream
- 1 cup whole milk
- 3/4 cup granulated sugar
- 5 large egg yolks
- 1 tsp vanilla extract
- 1/4 cup unsweetened cocoa powder
- 1/2 tsp ground cinnamon
- 1/4 cup cinnamon sugar (for swirling)

Instructions:

1. **Prepare the Custard:** Heat the cream, milk, and sugar in a saucepan. Whisk the egg yolks and temper with the warm cream mixture.
2. **Cook the Custard:** Return the mixture to the saucepan and cook until thickened. Strain and let it cool to room temperature.
3. **Add Cocoa Powder and Cinnamon:** Whisk the cocoa powder and cinnamon into the cooled custard along with the vanilla extract.
4. **Churn the Ice Cream:** Churn in an ice cream maker according to the manufacturer's instructions.
5. **Swirl Cinnamon Sugar:** Once the ice cream is almost frozen, swirl in the cinnamon sugar for a churro effect.
6. **Freeze and Serve:** Transfer to an airtight container and freeze for at least 4 hours before serving.

Raspberry Chocolate Swirl Ice Cream

Ingredients:

- 2 cups heavy cream
- 1 cup whole milk
- 3/4 cup granulated sugar
- 5 large egg yolks
- 1 tsp vanilla extract
- 1/2 cup raspberry puree
- 1/4 cup chocolate syrup

Instructions:

1. **Prepare the Custard:** Heat the cream, milk, and sugar in a saucepan. Whisk the egg yolks and temper with the warm cream mixture.
2. **Cook the Custard:** Return the mixture to the saucepan and cook until thickened. Strain and let it cool to room temperature.
3. **Churn the Ice Cream:** Churn the custard in an ice cream maker according to the manufacturer's instructions.
4. **Add Raspberry and Chocolate:** When the ice cream is almost frozen, swirl in the raspberry puree and chocolate syrup.
5. **Freeze and Serve:** Transfer to an airtight container and freeze for at least 4 hours before serving.

Vanilla Custard Ice Cream

Ingredients:

- 2 cups heavy cream
- 1 cup whole milk
- 3/4 cup granulated sugar
- 5 large egg yolks
- 1 vanilla bean, split and scraped (or 1 tbsp vanilla extract)

Instructions:

1. **Prepare the Custard Base:** Heat the cream, milk, and sugar in a saucepan until it starts to simmer. Whisk the egg yolks in a separate bowl.
2. **Temper the Eggs:** Slowly pour the hot cream mixture into the egg yolks while whisking constantly. Return the mixture to the saucepan and cook over medium heat, stirring constantly until thickened.
3. **Strain and Cool:** Remove from heat, strain the custard through a fine-mesh sieve to remove any curdled bits, and stir in the vanilla bean seeds or extract.
4. **Churn the Ice Cream:** Let the custard cool to room temperature, then refrigerate for several hours. Churn in an ice cream maker according to the manufacturer's instructions.
5. **Freeze and Serve:** Transfer to an airtight container and freeze for at least 4 hours before serving.

Maple Bacon Ice Cream

Ingredients:

- 2 cups heavy cream
- 1 cup whole milk
- 3/4 cup pure maple syrup
- 5 large egg yolks
- 1/2 tsp vanilla extract
- 6 slices bacon, cooked and crumbled

Instructions:

1. **Prepare the Custard Base:** Heat the cream, milk, and maple syrup in a saucepan. Whisk the egg yolks in a separate bowl.
2. **Temper the Eggs:** Slowly pour the hot cream mixture into the egg yolks while whisking constantly. Return the mixture to the saucepan and cook over medium heat, stirring constantly until thickened.
3. **Strain and Cool:** Strain the custard through a fine-mesh sieve and let it cool to room temperature. Stir in the vanilla extract.
4. **Churn the Ice Cream:** Once the custard has cooled, churn it in an ice cream maker according to the manufacturer's instructions.
5. **Add Bacon:** During the last few minutes of churning, add the crumbled bacon.
6. **Freeze and Serve:** Transfer to an airtight container and freeze for at least 4 hours before serving.

Black Forest Ice Cream

Ingredients:

- 2 cups heavy cream
- 1 cup whole milk
- 3/4 cup granulated sugar
- 5 large egg yolks
- 1 cup sour cherries, pitted and chopped
- 1/2 cup chocolate chips
- 1 tsp vanilla extract

Instructions:

1. **Prepare the Custard Base:** Heat the cream, milk, and sugar in a saucepan. Whisk the egg yolks in a separate bowl.
2. **Temper the Eggs:** Slowly pour the hot cream mixture into the egg yolks while whisking constantly. Return the mixture to the saucepan and cook over medium heat, stirring constantly until thickened.
3. **Strain and Cool:** Strain the custard through a fine-mesh sieve and let it cool to room temperature.
4. **Churn the Ice Cream:** Once the custard has cooled, churn it in an ice cream maker according to the manufacturer's instructions.
5. **Add Cherries and Chocolate:** During the last few minutes of churning, add the chopped cherries, chocolate chips, and vanilla extract.
6. **Freeze and Serve:** Transfer to an airtight container and freeze for at least 4 hours before serving.

Cherry Almond Ice Cream

Ingredients:

- 2 cups heavy cream
- 1 cup whole milk
- 3/4 cup granulated sugar
- 5 large egg yolks
- 1 cup fresh or frozen cherries, pitted and chopped
- 1/4 cup sliced almonds, toasted
- 1 tsp almond extract

Instructions:

1. **Prepare the Custard Base:** Heat the cream, milk, and sugar in a saucepan. Whisk the egg yolks in a separate bowl.
2. **Temper the Eggs:** Slowly pour the hot cream mixture into the egg yolks while whisking constantly. Return the mixture to the saucepan and cook over medium heat, stirring constantly until thickened.
3. **Strain and Cool:** Strain the custard through a fine-mesh sieve and let it cool to room temperature.
4. **Churn the Ice Cream:** Once the custard has cooled, churn it in an ice cream maker according to the manufacturer's instructions.
5. **Add Cherries and Almonds:** During the last few minutes of churning, add the chopped cherries, sliced almonds, and almond extract.
6. **Freeze and Serve:** Transfer to an airtight container and freeze for at least 4 hours before serving.

Green Tea Matcha Ice Cream

Ingredients:

- 2 cups heavy cream
- 1 cup whole milk
- 3/4 cup granulated sugar
- 5 large egg yolks
- 2 tbsp matcha green tea powder
- 1 tsp vanilla extract

Instructions:

1. **Prepare the Custard Base:** Heat the cream, milk, and sugar in a saucepan. Whisk the egg yolks in a separate bowl.
2. **Temper the Eggs:** Slowly pour the hot cream mixture into the egg yolks while whisking constantly. Return the mixture to the saucepan and cook over medium heat, stirring constantly until thickened.
3. **Strain and Cool:** Strain the custard through a fine-mesh sieve and let it cool to room temperature.
4. **Whisk in Matcha:** Once the custard has cooled, whisk in the matcha green tea powder and vanilla extract until smooth.
5. **Churn the Ice Cream:** Churn in an ice cream maker according to the manufacturer's instructions.
6. **Freeze and Serve:** Transfer to an airtight container and freeze for at least 4 hours before serving.

Caramel Pretzel Ice Cream

Ingredients:

- 2 cups heavy cream
- 1 cup whole milk
- 3/4 cup granulated sugar
- 5 large egg yolks
- 1/2 cup caramel sauce
- 1 cup crushed pretzels
- 1 tsp vanilla extract

Instructions:

1. **Prepare the Custard Base:** Heat the cream, milk, and sugar in a saucepan. Whisk the egg yolks in a separate bowl.
2. **Temper the Eggs:** Slowly pour the hot cream mixture into the egg yolks while whisking constantly. Return the mixture to the saucepan and cook over medium heat, stirring constantly until thickened.
3. **Strain and Cool:** Strain the custard through a fine-mesh sieve and let it cool to room temperature.
4. **Add Caramel:** Stir in the caramel sauce and vanilla extract.
5. **Churn the Ice Cream:** Churn the custard in an ice cream maker according to the manufacturer's instructions.
6. **Add Pretzels:** During the last few minutes of churning, add the crushed pretzels.
7. **Freeze and Serve:** Transfer to an airtight container and freeze for at least 4 hours before serving.

Coconut Chocolate Chip Ice Cream

Ingredients:

- 2 cups heavy cream
- 1 cup coconut milk
- 3/4 cup granulated sugar
- 5 large egg yolks
- 1/2 cup shredded coconut
- 1/2 cup mini chocolate chips
- 1 tsp vanilla extract

Instructions:

1. **Prepare the Custard Base:** Heat the cream, coconut milk, and sugar in a saucepan. Whisk the egg yolks in a separate bowl.
2. **Temper the Eggs:** Slowly pour the hot cream mixture into the egg yolks while whisking constantly. Return the mixture to the saucepan and cook over medium heat, stirring constantly until thickened.
3. **Strain and Cool:** Strain the custard through a fine-mesh sieve and let it cool to room temperature.
4. **Add Coconut:** Stir in the shredded coconut and vanilla extract.
5. **Churn the Ice Cream:** Churn the custard in an ice cream maker according to the manufacturer's instructions.
6. **Add Chocolate Chips:** During the last few minutes of churning, add the mini chocolate chips.
7. **Freeze and Serve:** Transfer to an airtight container and freeze for at least 4 hours before serving.

Brown Sugar Cinnamon Ice Cream

Ingredients:

- 2 cups heavy cream
- 1 cup whole milk
- 3/4 cup brown sugar
- 5 large egg yolks
- 1 tsp ground cinnamon
- 1 tsp vanilla extract

Instructions:

1. **Prepare the Custard Base:** Heat the cream, milk, and brown sugar in a saucepan until it begins to simmer. Whisk the egg yolks in a separate bowl.
2. **Temper the Eggs:** Slowly pour the hot cream mixture into the egg yolks while whisking constantly. Return the mixture to the saucepan and cook over medium heat, stirring constantly until thickened.
3. **Strain and Cool:** Strain the custard through a fine-mesh sieve and let it cool to room temperature.
4. **Add Cinnamon and Vanilla:** Stir in the ground cinnamon and vanilla extract.
5. **Churn the Ice Cream:** Churn the custard in an ice cream maker according to the manufacturer's instructions.
6. **Freeze and Serve:** Transfer to an airtight container and freeze for at least 4 hours before serving.

Toffee Almond Ice Cream

Ingredients:

- 2 cups heavy cream
- 1 cup whole milk
- 3/4 cup granulated sugar
- 5 large egg yolks
- 1/2 cup toffee bits
- 1/4 cup toasted almonds, chopped
- 1 tsp vanilla extract

Instructions:

1. **Prepare the Custard Base:** Heat the cream, milk, and sugar in a saucepan until it starts to simmer. Whisk the egg yolks in a separate bowl.
2. **Temper the Eggs:** Slowly pour the hot cream mixture into the egg yolks while whisking constantly. Return the mixture to the saucepan and cook over medium heat, stirring constantly until thickened.
3. **Strain and Cool:** Strain the custard through a fine-mesh sieve and let it cool to room temperature.
4. **Churn the Ice Cream:** Once the custard has cooled, churn it in an ice cream maker according to the manufacturer's instructions.
5. **Add Toffee and Almonds:** During the last few minutes of churning, add the toffee bits, chopped almonds, and vanilla extract.
6. **Freeze and Serve:** Transfer to an airtight container and freeze for at least 4 hours before serving.

Honeycomb Ice Cream

Ingredients:

- 2 cups heavy cream
- 1 cup whole milk
- 3/4 cup granulated sugar
- 5 large egg yolks
- 1/2 cup honeycomb candy, chopped into small pieces
- 1 tsp vanilla extract

Instructions:

1. **Prepare the Custard Base:** Heat the cream, milk, and sugar in a saucepan until it begins to simmer. Whisk the egg yolks in a separate bowl.
2. **Temper the Eggs:** Slowly pour the hot cream mixture into the egg yolks while whisking constantly. Return the mixture to the saucepan and cook over medium heat, stirring constantly until thickened.
3. **Strain and Cool:** Strain the custard through a fine-mesh sieve and let it cool to room temperature.
4. **Churn the Ice Cream:** Once the custard has cooled, churn it in an ice cream maker according to the manufacturer's instructions.
5. **Add Honeycomb:** During the last few minutes of churning, add the chopped honeycomb pieces and vanilla extract.
6. **Freeze and Serve:** Transfer to an airtight container and freeze for at least 4 hours before serving.

Gingerbread Ice Cream

Ingredients:

- 2 cups heavy cream
- 1 cup whole milk
- 3/4 cup brown sugar
- 5 large egg yolks
- 1 tsp ground ginger
- 1/2 tsp ground cinnamon
- 1/4 tsp ground cloves
- 1 tsp vanilla extract

Instructions:

1. **Prepare the Custard Base:** Heat the cream, milk, and brown sugar in a saucepan until it starts to simmer. Whisk the egg yolks in a separate bowl.
2. **Temper the Eggs:** Slowly pour the hot cream mixture into the egg yolks while whisking constantly. Return the mixture to the saucepan and cook over medium heat, stirring constantly until thickened.
3. **Strain and Cool:** Strain the custard through a fine-mesh sieve and let it cool to room temperature.
4. **Add Spices and Vanilla:** Stir in the ground ginger, cinnamon, cloves, and vanilla extract.
5. **Churn the Ice Cream:** Once the custard has cooled, churn it in an ice cream maker according to the manufacturer's instructions.
6. **Freeze and Serve:** Transfer to an airtight container and freeze for at least 4 hours before serving.

Chocolate Coconut Ice Cream

Ingredients:

- 2 cups heavy cream
- 1 cup coconut milk
- 3/4 cup granulated sugar
- 5 large egg yolks
- 1/2 cup unsweetened cocoa powder
- 1/2 cup shredded coconut
- 1 tsp vanilla extract

Instructions:

1. **Prepare the Custard Base:** Heat the cream, coconut milk, and sugar in a saucepan until it starts to simmer. Whisk the egg yolks in a separate bowl.
2. **Add Cocoa Powder:** Stir the cocoa powder into the hot cream mixture until fully dissolved.
3. **Temper the Eggs:** Slowly pour the hot cream mixture into the egg yolks while whisking constantly. Return the mixture to the saucepan and cook over medium heat, stirring constantly until thickened.
4. **Strain and Cool:** Strain the custard through a fine-mesh sieve and let it cool to room temperature.
5. **Churn the Ice Cream:** Once the custard has cooled, churn it in an ice cream maker according to the manufacturer's instructions.
6. **Add Coconut:** During the last few minutes of churning, add the shredded coconut and vanilla extract.
7. **Freeze and Serve:** Transfer to an airtight container and freeze for at least 4 hours before serving.

Vanilla Bean Bourbon Ice Cream

Ingredients:

- 2 cups heavy cream
- 1 cup whole milk
- 3/4 cup granulated sugar
- 5 large egg yolks
- 1 vanilla bean, split and scraped (or 1 tbsp vanilla extract)
- 2 tbsp bourbon

Instructions:

1. **Prepare the Custard Base:** Heat the cream, milk, and sugar in a saucepan until it starts to simmer. Whisk the egg yolks in a separate bowl.
2. **Temper the Eggs:** Slowly pour the hot cream mixture into the egg yolks while whisking constantly. Return the mixture to the saucepan and cook over medium heat, stirring constantly until thickened.
3. **Strain and Cool:** Strain the custard through a fine-mesh sieve and let it cool to room temperature.
4. **Add Bourbon and Vanilla:** Stir in the vanilla bean seeds (or extract) and bourbon.
5. **Churn the Ice Cream:** Once the custard has cooled, churn it in an ice cream maker according to the manufacturer's instructions.
6. **Freeze and Serve:** Transfer to an airtight container and freeze for at least 4 hours before serving.

Apple Cinnamon Ice Cream

Ingredients:

- 2 cups heavy cream
- 1 cup whole milk
- 3/4 cup granulated sugar
- 5 large egg yolks
- 1 cup cooked and mashed apples
- 1 tsp ground cinnamon
- 1 tsp vanilla extract

Instructions:

1. **Prepare the Custard Base:** Heat the cream, milk, and sugar in a saucepan until it starts to simmer. Whisk the egg yolks in a separate bowl.
2. **Temper the Eggs:** Slowly pour the hot cream mixture into the egg yolks while whisking constantly. Return the mixture to the saucepan and cook over medium heat, stirring constantly until thickened.
3. **Strain and Cool:** Strain the custard through a fine-mesh sieve and let it cool to room temperature.
4. **Add Apples, Cinnamon, and Vanilla:** Stir in the mashed apples, ground cinnamon, and vanilla extract.
5. **Churn the Ice Cream:** Once the custard has cooled, churn it in an ice cream maker according to the manufacturer's instructions.
6. **Freeze and Serve:** Transfer to an airtight container and freeze for at least 4 hours before serving.

www.ingramcontent.com/pod-product-compliance
Lightning Source LLC
LaVergne TN
LVHW081339060526
838201LV00055B/2740